100 Poems

100
Poems

JOHN FAIRFAX

Phoenix Press
1992

Phoenix Press
Hermitage, Newbury,
Berks RG16 9XR

ISBN 0 900852 13 5

Set in 10 point Palatino
by KMA Typesetting
Hartland, N. Devon

Printed in England by
Antony Rowe Limited, Chippenham, Wiltshire

Cover & Design, John Moat
Cover illustration from Eglise St-Pierre, Chauvigny
Photograph of John Fairfax, Michael Campbell Cole

Acknowledgement is due to the following magazines:

Outposts; Panache; Paris Review; Poetry Review; Spectator; Time and Tide; T.L.S.; Two Cities, Malahat Review; Temenos; Interactions; Acumen; Other Poetry; Illuminations; Anglo Welsh Review; Pearl; Psychopoetica; Neuropa; Prospice; BBC radio; Resurgence; South West Review.

Phoenix Press acknowledges financial assistance from Southern Arts.

Contents

A geography of fire
Brands on an oak log,
Huge as a thigh,
Those enchanting shapes
From the barbary coast
That I see in the wood
Through prism of a tear
That dries on my cheek
As I dream before the blaze.

THIS I SAY

Waverider

Reach out waverider on an ocean
To where drowned seamen
Heave their keel in a requiem
Of reefs.   Dismasted
In a decide of sinking
They ride out a storm
In a cockleshell of love.
Attempt an ocean. Navigate
Adventure in a whirl of water
Going places without end
On winds trading between
Those in peril and beneath a sea.

Once I Saw The Space

Once I saw the space
Of procreation
Between the bird face
Flight and migration.

This the autumn gave
To furled distance
That the movements have
Stopped in their dance.

The Zennor Road
for George Barker

Late and the getting later moon calls
After a poet who grabs at the sky
And on his knees, stumbling drunk,
Prays for Li Po's immortal soul.

Birch Cottage

On a hill in a landscape of trees
The cottage like a colourful weed
Among corn blooms in the sun.
Wander soft-treading pine weave
Through those tall wood fingers:
And in a mist eyed second
Falter while pigeons burst
Skyward, hares crackle gorse
Away to fern, pheasants explode
A bush in brilliant fear.
And see my cottage resolute
As a boulder atop a hill.

A Boy And A Rabbit

Running as untamed as the sky
Along highways of grass a rabbit,
Halted by a poacher's ring, was killed.
The poacher, a boy unknown to death,
Saw his own road gold with traps.
Watching his prey's eyes dead,
With questions transfixed for reply,
The boy crying at his power
Took the rabbit home and lay
That death on a board. He drew the figure
Answering its eyes and head
In the colour of his defeat.

THE 5TH HORSEMAN OF THE APOCALYPSE

(lines 361-412 & 510-end)

And still the fifth horseman
Plods, seen by one or two,
Seen through by one or two;
Ignored and missed
By the green spiel
Cantillation of free offers
To slavery and suicide.

The magnet of gold
Splendours and gifts of myrrh
Pursue a star
Until in place
Of gorgeous
Venus or Aphrodite

A hag with eight dugs
Embraces you
Burying hollow fangs
Into your ripped throat.
And the box you watch
Is full of dogdreams,
Is full of worms
Eating at your bones.

A scream you ache
Bursts out as a jingle;
And the fist you beat
Is covered by kid skin.
And the tear welling
Through your eye
Is prescribed
In the gibbering glibness
Of afternoon tea.

The fifth horseman passes
In the morning, noon,
Afternoon, and evening.
At night he passes.

The glow-worm
And nightingale
Is aware of the plot

And keep the sound and light
Alive, although you may
Only catch their life
From precarious cliff tops,
Or by deep river,
Or on wild moor.

The dark city woods and fields
And cottages and castles
Are full of imitation.
The seashore, desert,
Mountains, ocean, inland lakes
And millponds are full
Of manufactured light and sound
Dressed in the splendid
Mist of deception.

As the Black Horseman reared
And caught the scales
The fifth horseman passed.

At first the starvation
Was in the belly.
Ribs split skin
And stomach paunched,
Limbs unable to rise,
And eyes clawed,
The hunger a pursuit
Of food, a paper chase
For the wastage
Of entrails.

But the fifth
Horseman
Rode in the Black
Shadow and took the field
Where starvation eats at the unseeable.

Watch the fat and fulsome
Starve. Watch the rich
And powerful waste away.
The dreams go first,
The empty plate of dreams,
And then starvation begins.
The fifth horseman drags
Away truth and courage
And those abstractions
Which bleak on a page
Keep the juices of man
Alive, keep his ribs
Pliant and his belly tight.

The fifth horseman
Tramples the feeding
Abstractions underfoot
So that even swine may not
Eat thereof
And a man must die.

The fifth horseman rides
With his Black twin.

And then the last seal
Was broken and a Pale Horseman
Of hell cantered
Into the lists of the dark city.
The fifth horseman
Collected about him a mist
And a constantly changing
Shape.
In the lake,
On still oceans the reflection
Of the fifth horseman
Practises a Pale countenance
Of hell and rests and feeds
His Tarot nag at the stagnant
Pool of primal evil
Each hell will take on
In the blaring neon despair
Of the dark city
Where the lights become knife
Blades that cut to shreds
Those who follow to slavery
The neon light or the faking
Image enlarged to swallow hell.

Behind the image swirls a sea
Of the blood of men
Who were ridden down by the white
Hounds and chameleon horse
Of undying death's
Fifth horseman of the Apocalypse.

O horseman, O city.
O love. The ache is easy
To bare. Pass horseman.

I know you by the green
Poisoned hood, and blood

Red shirt you wear.
I know you
For honesty.

No prancing,
No pretending,
No word to encourage dreams.

You hold no flag aloft.
No promise.
Not even death.
Like the four kin horsemen
No revelation.

I see you fifth horseman
Trail the drooped shoulder
And the haunted eye
And the clenched jaw and fist.

I recognise the twist of lip
And the lowered head
Shielding your laser eye
That burns into and through
The white shroud
On which a projection
Plays excuses
For the brothers
Of Apocalypse.

SPACE POEMS

Oration for a Space Shot

Do not let your eyes be blinded
In the unfamiliar light
Of stars named cozily from
Greek and Roman Deities.

Where we are to the limits
Of no imagination
Is farther than we can think.

And the charts are treacherous
(As the Mappa Mundi skin)
For men to use faithfully.

The brittle egg you ride in
And voices that link the chain
Are guesses on blobs of ink.

That chain between long darkness
And daily exercise is
Forged in the furnace head of

Men like you and me. In love,
Hungry, fined for parking, drunk,
Listening, weary, mad; always

Fidgeting to another
Day. In the pursuit—of what?
The moon of course, and...and then

The next dominion away
In the unreached darkness.
Just take a look towards the

Sky for the emptiness you
See will be filed and filmed,
Recorded and analysed

Until it is a mystery
No longer, invisible
Only to the fleet planet

Changing before the hand can

Reach it, or the roaring boys
Empty their capsule of waste.

Go on. Chase on. Do not look
Too closely at the love in
Your arms, be blindly strong be

Out of the complex daily
Spit, be away from table
And chair, hoe and spade, voice, ear.

Go where the black sky has holes
For you to crawl through; and chart
Memory carried so far

That it grows like choking cords
Of birth, of life, and of death,
To atmospheres distant as

The concrete pads you sped from—
The mountains left behind that
Are breakfast, beer and skittles.

Do not let your eyes be blinded
In the unfamiliar light;
Take our smoked glass with you.

As most admirably, surely
You will until the sun
And the moon display patterns

On the inside of your egg
To break the computer will:
Fingered from a wood cabin

In the moon city of a
Continent filled with more push
Buttons than kisses. O rise,

O roar outward: we have not
Done better yet than explore
The emptiness between us

And the golden chains circling

Giant infertile, binding,
Eggs. Soar out brave boys your grail

Is filled with the blood of men,
A whole wretchedness of time,
Of men who gaze in mirrors,

Who look along the ocean,
Tap among dense trees towards
The next tree. Ride out brothers

I, too, am with you, armed
With the wish and will, footing
With dead poets at my side

The blank, blind, unknowable
Track of blood that leads, that leads,
Leads on to O god knows where.

Then it will be said that if
The planets you land upon
Had not been there it would be

Necessary for you to
Invent them. So make them be.
Each alien atmosphere will

Rise like a diamond flower
Touched by sunlight; and brought
Lightyears across the sky is

Man, vizored and gauntleted,
Pecking at the longshot crust
That hatches him everywhere.

12 Stations From Gemini

1

Dials indicate fable
Exploding
This shell into orbit.

Hand, eye, and tongue record
The spinning
Guess that is destiny.

2
Earth and sun, sun and earth
Pull me to
Them in quickening beauty.

From cave to capsule I
Swim weightless
To generate a star.

3
The long, long haul is on
Across void
Out into unthinkable

Space where men pursue
The anger
Of their image into gods.

4
I awake to the gold
Tint of light
That is my emblemed shield.

Gold shield, gold cord, anchor
Me to life
And precise blind gauges.

5
Around, up, forward, turn;
Movements call
Mind and blood, counting steps

That I take looking back
Along skies
That curve to forever.

6
Endlessly you and I
Move from or
To our deaths and issue.

24

Who will inherit stars?
My dust and
Theirs? Where, where are you?

7
This suit is not my skin,
This vein does
Not throb with my blood,

These teeth and nails will fall.
My eyes fail
In this golden vizor.

8
Yet I am here and proud.
O the awe
The wonderful threshold

Turning, turning away
In distances
My heart and mind will cross.

9
Do not build me a tomb,
Cast medal,
Or call streets by my name.

Out here memorial
Is nothing: dust
That collects about my head.

10
It is easier to
Withstand G
Than the piledriving death

That comes from remaining
Unarmed and
Afraid of changing stars.

11
Roaring towards nothing
But distant
Holes and wilder guesses

I'll lie here cramped, singing
To you who
Are deaf to the calling sky.

       12
For if stories are false
I'm with gods
Who either care or do not

Who or why or what I am,
And where I
Spin my stations for you.

The Black Fleece

Cast me an anchor at a star
Chart unknowable oceans,
Give me a crew of Argonauts
And I will map the skies.

Beyond moon, beyond the black
Are realms and riches, whole
Dreams. My saviour sapphire nails
I'll bring, and an emerald tomb.

For ships and food I'll press
A full rigged king. Come Jason
Hand me a rod and I'll break
A bright discipline of stars.

Beyond Astronaut

And out in the black chart
Our lightlives away ride the roaring
Boys who slide through space.

A universe of unmapped grief and love
And new master light is beyond
The pleiades and plough and southern stars.
Far sisters far behind, left standing

As lean lads gyrate, siren
Silent, through the bewildering sky.
See them take a superstition which makes
Endless the forever night of destiny
Beyond sight and measure.

O Soaring
Icarus of outworld, burn bright
The traceries of known skymarks,
Slide the highway planets behind
Your clear waxed wings.

Go conquer the everywhere left
Beyond your sad confinement
In a predicted bonehouse,
Witch thrown riddle of flesh
And water.

O soar until nothing
Remains but great glittering holes
In the black godspun shirt over your head.

All Adam Again

Spin, weave, whirl out there in a blind eye
Which like frosted window sees light
That is reflection from frozen furies
Thumping adrenalin of spheres to man,
One man composite of all love
And hate and Cain and brothers and murdered
And raped sisters, dying and dead, conceived
And crawling, evolving like minute life
Over the crowded summer beaches
Towards the picnic basket of the gods
Weekending from pressure of godliness;
From the known and undiademed days
White with ordinariness, or blue
With the sameness of brittle nags
That break into dreams and tease the white
Eyes to look, and fingers to trace
A new name on the blind deep frost
That is cheating vision. That is innocence

Gurgling wordless in a galactic cot,
Rattling the last swanlike wounds caressing
Itself in its own image.

Xist what a world
Is wonderful. What bounty abounds
In spinning, weaving, whirling history
That we look down with our tapping stick
And toppling legends.

O wonder
What a world is Xist. And now the march
Is hammering in the womb, the seeds
Are roaring at the rock. Put down sling,
Rifle, bomb and missile, you have lost.
Look up, look up, damn you, that darkness,
That abstraction you see is lapping
At seas you are the plankton crawling from.
All Adam again. Again. Courage.
What wonder. What awe. What bounty.

No more the close clinging fur to wrap
The bride and her lusting love, no swaddling
Lace for their issue. No more the flag
To rally with emblem lion, leaf, bird, bear.
The ranks will close. Close ranks. Join as one,
Be the wonder in the sky spinning,
Weaving, whirling, in the orgasmic
Moment that is kiss of life as capsules
Evolve in the bedchamber of stars.

From **The Sea of Tranquillity**
For John Moat

The sinews tighten as my head tilts back
To look at the sky; in particular the moon.
My eyes travel through the peels of Space
To those ancient bodies that might still be:
Although the moment I see started so long ago
That the light reflected in my eyes is older
Than my mind will calendar.

Now I
Hold with the bits of metal we throw up
Ranging orbits farther out each chance.
I watch the stars and divine weary Magi
With spinning gifts in foam-fitting couches;
And my voice is loud in the night and calls the capsules
In from their fragile hour on the Tranquil Sea.

Blue moon—harvest moon—lover's moon—man in the moon
Is superseded as of 20th February, 1965,
When Ranger Eight broke its back on a grey sea,
The Mare Tranquillitatis, and raised dust
That didn't get itself spat on and rolled
Into, harrowed, ploughed, sandcastled. The moon is different.

It now stares down with a foreign body
Like a thorn splinter just beneath the skin,
And a future likely to trick the past.

Old man, O moon, I saw you before the instrument
Pierced you, and I see you now. I almost feel the same
And honestly cannot decry your violation.
We are both different now, you and I.

I'm long glad
I don't have to ride a horse, saddle a brute;
But can tune twin-carbs and howl down a Clearway
When and where I wish as quickly as I choose.

The more there is around and on you, moon, the more
I speculate on machines and computers and am pleased
And grateful. It makes history an evolution.
And those fitting who had a hand in putting
The Eighth Ranger into the depthless dustful sea.
It makes the nails and lives and compassion and hero and coward
And God and tomb-robber, judged and judge,
The whole crazy unbalance of recorded man
A small piece of expensive engineering, dust covered,
On a coagulated gas we moon.

Moon that nights
And shows us where to put drunken feet
As we stagger from fire-sides to throw
Our heads back until the sinews in our necks tighten
And beneath our feet the orb is reflected
In a river we can touch: We can touch and embrace.

Orbiting Ark

120 frogs eggs and 64 blue spiderwort
were launched into earth orbit
in biosatellite 2.

The pepper seed in my pepper mill
favours adventure
knowing now that pepper grows
more quickly in the denser air
than it does on earth.
Flour beetles swell with cunning
pride having spun from Cape Kennedy
in the same satellite as wheat seedlings.
And have you noticed that wasps
are more purposeful this year?

The vinegar gnat abuzz in orbit
leaves the world a lesser place.
And the trip of endless bacteria
makes running noses astroprobe.
Bread and fishes weren't forgotten
10 million spore of orange bread mould
and floating amoebae
lived by a sea of strontium:
but the whole ark returned
to an insane dust man
who plans to make heaven
the same as earth.

One day a planetrider
might hear a plaintive croak
of a bullfrog
and imagine that the blue spiderwort
is spinning webs as quickly
as the capsule
in which he is incubating.

30

Moonsong

Rise through the sky
To the moon way above
I spin on my couch
From this Earth that I love.

O I will walk
On the grey tranquil sea
Casting no shadow
Seeking no mystery.

I'll gather dust
And some diamond rock
To give blue Earth
For her jealous stock.

Don't look for me
Singing over your head
Join the moonsong
And our freefalling tread.

Orpheus is here
In gold tinted dome,
Icarus left
On his long way home.

We have marked the track
Through orbital bar
And sung our way
To this lonely star.

Now raise your eyes
And your voice and your hands
The moon has danced
To Apollo's band.

O rise through space
To the stars way above
Spin on your couches
From the blue Earth you love.

BONE HARVEST DONE

A Stream Recalled

Steps from my childhood led
To a flagstone corridor—
Distorting mirror.
The corridor sloped
Steeply enough
For toys to race down.

The flagstones were cold blue.
Sometimes they sang.

In winter they hissed, and a rime
Shimmered along the corridor.
Those days I hurried through the place
To warm rooms.
Each day sealed its temper on me
Echoing my heel tap.

Beneath the stones on summer days
There were finger bells
That teased me to kneel and listen
Until into my head that stream,
Under the hallway of my boyhood,
Etched deep runs.
Even now I hear it when I listen.

I remember one room in
The house was silent.
That was my parents' room.
I barely knew it—the quiet
Was its lock.

They are fixed behind the mirror
Of that childhood
By their separate stairway,
Dark door;
Their tall and hollow room.

They could not read
The flagstones
Nor dream the corridor
Nor hear my Devon stream.

Once I clambered rocks of returning
To find only blue flagstones
Bridging a stream below a hallway.

Yet I think I know the shadow
I caught kneeling to hear the water.
I see a boy listen when I listen.

Fantasy for a Child

I remember a track between the trees
My ash stick that cut down the thorn
And sliced the gold-headed flowers,
And moved a stone beneath the water
Of a stream I remember now:
Against a ruined wall and broken tree
I remember those bubbling years.

Companions never lost their way.
I remember following the moon to the sea
Down a corridor of boulders and night,
My hair grasped by the hard hand of an oak;
I remember, and so do they.

I remember a flight across the land—
Whether a dream or mine.
I remember the waiting; and commands
That ran like water in my ears.
I remember fishing from a boat.

I walked with the trees and sun,
With my ash stick and my laughter
Away from the market and the noise
Of tears, and business that was not mine.
I remember the motionless air and am glad.

I remember a grove and sleeping friends
And night, flames, feeling like thieves
And hanging like them in the shadows,
Until I became one and was caught
Beneath the trees because friends slept.

I remember the ash stick and the thorns,
Green thorns whirling from a hedge
And flowers falling golden on the grass.
I remember a summer of birds and sky of trees
That have died and now die with me.

We are Three

Guess. That trailing mark is written
Above every cot before the child is there,
Bells ring and candles light the to-bed stairs.
A storm, closed, hand in glove,
Quails under dividing hands, and is conveyed
From Orion's belt and from the plough,
From the little sister at the telephone,
Caesars in Cleopatra beds, spaniels
With celtic eyes, and from kittens with wool.
Quail, wisemen, there the proverb plays.
Bright mouth on my sore shoulder. Sleep.

I dream my time away, and watch
The fishes among watergrass and birds
Among a sky of trees, animals among themselves,
And all that move and can be watched.
But mostly I dream. The words
Follow. The grief is there. It is
Blossoming to a death. Hands, feet and head
Deep in the grave. But that question
Repeats: We are three, we are three?
Resounding like a silence in every ear.

February Morning

I dream through this winter of mist and gossamer.
Calm from the season engrosses my wood.
Spring is weeks away.

Magpie, crow and pheasant no longer stir the air
With harsh cry and frightened wing beating the wind.
A mist heavy with ice is adding frozen tracery
To sleeping limb of hazel, holly, laurel and beech.

As I walk over white brittle grass I hear
But cannot see bunched cattle scraping pasture,
Can hear distant ploughs turning iron furrows
Until the tractor stops and silence is full.

The wood I walk is close as the unmoving winter
Of this February morning. Down a rhododendron track
I pass with my hands warm in my pockets to where
A pheasant caught in a keeper's trap breaks the quiet
As she thrusts at the netting, losing feathers in fear.

In this black month the trap is harmless,
It is there to collect her to mother another brood
To feed next autumn sport. I go by and she settles
To eat the crop that trapped her.

A grey squirrel
Perches on a bole of an oak taking no notice as I pass—
No screwing scamper along branches, no anxious leap—
It sits motionless. The people of Eling Wood and winter
Are thickblooded through this frozen morning.

Even late gossamer from bramble to bracken is unbroken;
And as I walk deeper among the trees I am affected
To move with care. With care I breathe and walk
As, I too, await the Spring.

Song of the Wind

For Michael Campbell-Cole

I will accompany the wind
Over mountain
And through gold field:
I will tease spray
From tall wave crest.
O I will accompany the wind.

Riding a song
In every ear:
Among city street
In lonely room,
I will accompany the wind.

O I will accompany the wind
Until the chain
Of my white bones
Drifts like fine sand
And I become compassing wind.

And I become the wind.

Prelude for Michael

March in the mad Spring from my cottage
Sped and touched eyehills with a blackened hand.
Come, Michael, beside our tall, tall fir,
Spread your three years over a spell as fast
As the beaten babes kissed by winter.
What your inheritance I cannot guess.

A moth like time beats at the window
That you must ride master out all your days.
Michael, draw your bow and kiss the gut.
Be sure. Loose the bolt and pin the gold.
Welcome your days with a memory
Of unlikely Pentecosts. Michael remember

March is mad, seasons are your margin.
Armour yourself for war with a fistful
Of dreaming dust always in the hand,
Both false and flourishing. Come, Michael,
Here by our cottage. It was here we talked
Of invisible one, and what will be.

For Jonathan

Down, down the bright slide of day
The enlarging sun careers
Through geographies. And, at last,
Bled crimson, rests
Beneath the hills, beyond the woods
Where only you, my babe, shall play.

Lines for Esther, August 30

On each other we have sprung a decade of love;
And I see my sons among birch trees
Stretch from our bed. We could not celebrate
In beer and meat our matrimonial day
For lack of cash, but my love, we have kicked
The backside of mortgage and loose
Couches for ten years which makes my verse
To you the ring we did not need of gold.

As I remember we joined on a wet day,
A Chinese meal and a curtain ring.
Our beds have been bare but of our choice,
And you from tears to both sons had faith
When stolen food eased the boys' bellies.
Have this address of my love, Esther, which I know
You do not need in words as our love spills
Over verb and gift and grief of possession.

At a Seawall

Tonight alone at a seawall
I hear her song
And the island spins.

She dances circles in the tide
Which flows and falls combed
Through her hair.

She holds wave and breaker then pours
Them from her hand
To pearl the rock.

As night parts the battered stars
Catch the white hem
Of her frail dress.

Tonight alone at a seawall
I reach for her hand and the cry
Of gulls deafens me.

O I know her in white water,
In green sea, in storming water.
I know her touch.

She hums a rockabye
Picks chords on every surf
And frets the sand.

She sighs in depth and shallow,
Rages sea at fringed bay,
Blinds me with gazing.

Tonight alone at a seawall
The moon and I stare
While one awake cries.

The shore changes. Seabirds ride
And feed alone on sea-surge.
She haunts my song.

She calls me but I cannot go.
I made this seawall
Where alone tonight I listen.

Mountains Sing

Mountains sing and oceans whistle.
What wife weaves one coloured cotton?
And say what woodsman clips from one tree;
Not me.

I took a rose while walking
And the bee lost his honey.
He had three,
O he had three,
But the bee lost his honey.

And now there are two stings
in me
And now there are two stings
in me.

I cannot shout that the lyric lie decayed

I cannot shout that the lyric lie decayed
On a latitude pursued by a spring moon,
Cannot silently shift my pen protesting
Against a frogthroated minstrel who is unwired
Without a skeleton of a harp. Listen.
The rain objects, and the wind is out of tune,
The bee hums flat and the wasp is hopping mad
As the fugue flowers allow. Lyric lie decay.

Today while I rested at my door I heard
An infant and an old man talking in verse.
This is spring when that may happen.
And it did. And still the lyric lie decayed.
I did not see a brand of fire spit flame
At the sea nor did I see a mountain dance.
But this was a dream heart hung with my anger.
And as they walked on through the mouth of a hill
I followed, as though called by a pied player.
I do not say that the lyric lie decayed.

Bone Harvest Done

Speak: for who can say
Where the farthest star clings,
Or the sun unlooses day,
Or a dead blue Jay swings?

September covers summer
And flesh crawls under wool,
The sky, an insane drummer,
Beats down my winter fuel.

O speak: for who can say
Come with me? Who will give
Hand warmth to a child's play
Against nightmares that live?

Abed in unkicked leaves
The babes dress in their grief
And autumns, dark as thieves,
Make their comfort brief.

Bone harvest done: they swear
Death lasts. Be sure to die,
It is all you live to bear
Since broken hearts must lie.

O speak: for who can say
Where the farthest star clings
Or the sun unlooses day,
Or a dead blue Jay swings?

Live apace upon a hill,
Break against a northern wind,
Feel them turn on you to kill
Because you love: and love sinned.

A child in autumn sapped
And stretched a harvest hand
Full of words night lapped
For the bright wings that fanned

Before they died to hang
On a wire fence. And you walk
Shouting at what dared to gang
Against you—sparrow riled hawk?

Sprinkle out, break or bow out,
Prettier than you were kicked
By the transparent lout
Flouncing the ones he picked

To wheel screeching gullwise
Over Nomansland. Turn stone,
Shoulder sky, the dead disguise
Themselves in wind-white bone.

O speak: for who can say
Where the farthest star clings,
Or the sun unlooses day,
Or a dead blue Jay swings?

Star Spurred

The tale is told my words have gone
With wind and spindrift up along

The valley from the sea's dry line
To where like cinnamon brackens shine

At the moon's lowering eye
Softlanding tears of goodbye.

I'll hum no tune by water edge
Unless my love in silent pledge

Will know my flight is curling through
The warrens of her loving too;

And hold, although I must depart,
The broken measure of our heart.

As I look back so salt appears
Carving figures from my tears.

My ear picks at the rhyming of
A swinging gate or sleeping dove

And hears the water of the stream
Lulling a dragonfly to dream.

No matter from where nor how far
I'll chart the circle of my star

Back to this valley by the shore
To clasp the hand of love once more

And for a season of delight
Will flower a stillness in the night.

Three Swallows

They came late
three of them
stitching holes in
the summer air.
An equinox shivered
above the bee-
laden buddleia.

Early summer
the bees had it
their way sucking
out the golden
baubles of July:
hiving a clear
run between
nectar and cell.

Minutes tally
each latitude,
divided hemispheres
pilot swallows
whose auguries
turn seasons
into flight.

The air awoke
alive to swallows
drawing a fine net
of sky down
towards full rose,
columbine, bramble,
and setting apple.

Over the thatch
and buddleia
three swallows rake
honey heavy bees
in a summer haul.
From my shed
three swallows
punctuate my summer.

Stages from a Lamenting Tongue

1
Along a wordless parabola
I multiplied days
And found no escape:
Until a golden spur urged me
Headlong towards the moon
On a trajectory computed
In my pulse.

I drifted endless roads
And nameless towns
Until my flight was arrested.

An echo raged in my head.
No tongue could I find
For the thundering of my ears.

I came to the lap of an ocean
And my journey ended (and began).
I fingered a sea of tears
And laughter—a sea of chaos
And tranquillity. There in dream I saw
My oarless coracle spinning.

2
Songs echoing from rock
Broke into my skull and against
My ribs shaking this frame
As though nothing but dry leaves
And moondust were alive in me.

By Atlantic water and hewn cliff,
By river and at the root of the oak,
In word-freezing air and snapping
Moonshafts, I have listened to song

Then at last the sea sang.
A dog ran, a hand reached out,
The winds shifted in my ears
And words—heat shielded—
Dropped from my tongue
And their silence deafened me.

I grew in shadow
Until a blade of light
Burned at my lips
And I called your name
Down a history
Of anguished bone
To douse the pain.
Yet no rhythm could break
My silence.

3
I looked into the waters
Of each stone bridge I found
And watched the boulders move.
I felt a sword in my hand
Thrust and twist on bone.
I learned the cunning of the gull
In flight against wind and cliff.
I caught the dialogue of seasons
And counted each breath.
I was amazed as the head
Of Apollo floated in a red collar
On an Ocean.........calling.

The poets sang. They heard and sang.
I saw a striped shroud mark
The bobbing skull.
Then I heard that death
Was all about: in every wavelength
In every calculation,
In every deed;
In the hand of love clasped
To the hand of love.

4
The first cold hand to clasp mine
On the night-rock
Dragged words from my lips
But the white sea wave
And winter wind cut
All verbs I called
Until in silence I returned

To my path treading shadow
Cast by the moon on the road
I walk.

My first song was for the sea
(to ease my fear), no cathedral,
No odyssey, no spectral love.
The alphabet I played
Was a syllable for death.
And having sung in silence
To night-breakers by the shore
I saw the moon turn tail
And disappear.

5
I followed a black hag winding
Through halls of distorting glass
And knew at last that only by a token
Between each heart
Is there chain enough to bind
A love and life
On blazing rock where eyes deceive.

6
And only words called each to each
Are tokens, from one skull to another,
Holding vigil beneath the skin
As a vacant shell and mask
Is circling and aloud with stars.

I call.   I call.
My pulse is requiem
That must salve wounds
I cannot bind
Until I hear a hymn
From the white rose
As I pass by your summer grave.

ADRIFT ON THE STAR BROW OF TALIESIN

Renewing Riddle

I have been the sharp blade of a sword
I have been the wound I made.

I have been a gasp of air
And I have been a gale.

I have been a distant star
I have walked in darkness.

I have been a word everywhere
And the first sound uttered.

I have been a light cast on a wall
And a shadow in a cave.

I have been a river
And the bridge across it.

I have been an eagle
Hidden in the highest mountain.

I have commanded in battle
I have been victor and victim.

I have been sounding board
And the strings of a harp.

I have been meshed in silken
Nets in the sea; and have learnt.

There is nothing I have not been—
Now I am of land and sea and sky.

I have been many shapes
Before I became Taliesin.

Elan Valley

for Kit and Ilse

Hide of cattle, feather of fowl,
Granite of hill and wild mountain,
Lonely, lonely, lovely Elan.

To see, to live, is to be breath
On ice, tear in a storm of rain: is man
Among autumn rising in your long voice.

Little Song

On the land an oak will grow
On a bough an owl may stand
From lasting clouds a rain will fall
Upon the earth to water seed.

Each to each returns its need
To act upon the other's call
No locking ring may stay the hand
Nor halt the seasons as they flow.

Fathering Song

I listen for my infant's cry
Watching crows peck at the sky.

I feel the knife pare to bone
See blood leaking from a stone.

I weave a circle of lilting song
Marking depths where roots belong.

At my hall near this lake
Waters of my life must break.

Again again bloodbirds fly
Along the rainbows of my eye.

Candle Song

Where foot falls
Where hands rest
Where tears spring
Where love bounds

Where cinders blaze
Where sunlight warms
Where raindrops feed
Where seedling grows

A ring repeats
Its turning on
An endless song
In candle light.

Taliesin Sees

Taliesin sees because his eyes
Seek beyond a covering of mist,
Because his blood pumps a heritage
That turns turtle to the calendar.

The beginning was so long ago
That it can join with tomorrow
Through an endless ring of seasons
Filled with howls and mirth between.

Taliesin sees.
The water in this muddy pool
Is no less the same as covered
Gods beyond the eyes of time
Recorded in rain on stone today.

Today is yesterday repeated
Tomorrow and tomorrow until
Each new season invents
Its fall, and grace is granted

One to one by hand and mouth
From father to son, son to father

Until no lie can issue
From the broken eye: Then
May
The
Circling
Stop.

Taliesin Crosses a River

Long ago the valley was narrow
Cropped grass and large boulders
Charted the meadow, on my right
Hand side a river trebled
A mere stride to cross.

I had cast aside sacking and cowshed
My tongue parted my lips.
Through my teeth songs daggered
And took shape in the air.
At the beginning my valley was restless.

I found colour for my cloak
And skimmed verbs on quiet water.
I turned my eyes into acorn and leaf.
I ran under poppies from blackbirds,
I swung on the meadow grass.

There was no loneness. She was rib
Supple with love to lullaby boulders
Rocked without moving into all years.
The meadow moved. The valley widened.
And the river grew.

My song formed within a dream
Peopling the restless valley,
Cutting highways in atlased meadow,
Seeking release in oceaned river—
And the water stretched a vault wide.

Taliesin sang and drew his cloak
Over his shoulders—over every thing.
And every thing stayed an instant

Until the I of the poem ripped out
And spells were cast around.

I was the mindless valley
I was the grass curled into winds
I was unmoving boulder
I was the song, and the sound
Of the water of the river.

The colour of my cloak whitened
My tongue pinned magic in word
My rib stiffened and my eyes
Ceased looking to see deep
Into the tricking river.

Debris and blood bunched skin of water
Which on my right hand side
Was now and evermore, forever wide.
Valley slope flattened beyond seeing.
I, Taliesin, tapped at the boulder

And the rock answered back.
'Cross the river. There is nothing here
For a song.' And there was no end
To the water. Liquid the bank.
Liquid the crushed grass.

I turned to air and water creatures
But none could bridge me
The bridge of wounds over meadow river
That licked at my feet as though on fire.
I stood at a boulder and sang.

The song held. I felt the boulder move.
The song held. The river blazed
Beyond flame. I felt the boulder crack.
My song choked on blood.
The boulder.....

A song trickled through the wound
Like a meadow river beginning
A hop wide. Restless valley settled,
Grass solved riddles and boulder shaped
Rib and rock.
Taliesin crossed the river.

Circle of Gold

November frost glistens in his eye.
Taliesin pulls his chief cloak
About his shoulders.

Inside the hood all stars direct
Galaxies and around the hem
Leviathans renew one another.

Cradled in his arms Taliesin
Holds an infant sleeping as the fireblaze
Plays radiance on his smooth brow.

He rocks and hums with november
And feels restless movement
As the child wakes and stirs.

Folds of six colours drape
About his tall oak chair
As poet and babe gaze into the fire.

Then images flicker from the hearth
Around the walls, and along curling
Gold thread in the poet's cloak.

Two tongues pick at a tune
Softly joined in shadowed light
Until as one it leaves the lips.

Taliesin's head is hidden in the hood,
His feet are firm on flagstone,
While out of his skull

Sounds drop plain to hear.
The child moves in his arms
Eyes radiant and eagerly shifting.

Strong fingers pick at the cloak
Unravelling a thread from the weave,
Unwinding the first circle of gold.

Outside november night gathers
With a harmony of autumn leaves
Blown down a wind.

Quietly by the fire Taliesin
Humming from within his closing hood
Places the seeing child on to a chair.

And the glowing head is clothed
In a vestment with bright
Colours spreading.

Together two voices rise
Until at the end of breath one soars
And one falls away......echoing.

WILD CHILDREN

Wild children

Everywhere, plain, savanna, desert,
Mountain valley, forest, jungle,
Open space, or enclosed thicket,
Outside the cluttered skull
Experiences me.

My kin are fallen from nomadic
Carriers left to bleach on sand
Or where they lie. Some adopt
An aspect of grass.
Changeling survives.

What we do not know or understand
Distracts us. In my living
There is no past nor any future.
As I wake or sleep is all one.
Light and dark limit me.

My tongue is tuned about me,
My voice changes pitch and meaning.
I have been wolf-boy of Kronstadt,
I have been bear girl of Karpfen:
And alone, alone. Aveyron.

I keep pace with Sahara gazelle
And follow law of pack and herd.
Under fur and muscle I live
Nudging my way for crop or kill—
And at the waterhole.

Still, so still, my changing skin quivers
And my eyes picture things inward I
Cannot understand, cannot growl at,
Cannot leap or run from, can only glimpse
Against sky, water, or forest tree.

I have lived as wolf, as bear, as pig,
As monkey, ostrich, as leopard, as gazelle,
With these I have known. And there is more,
O so much more. Both before now, now. Now
And. . . .

I curl in a womb. I kneel
Before the altered aspect of my gods:
Into whom am I seeking to change?
One by one my identities bloom
That one shall flower.

I have been run to death. Poisoned. Starved.
Neglected. Confined. I have been trodden
Down and hoisted by the neck.
I have acted thus.
I have been my own hunter.

I have been found. Netted. Trapped
And hamstrung. Exhibited. But I have begun again.
I changed. I fled. I broke the circle.
I have stared into the mirror
And escaped.

Wolf child

Know me in wolf den
Among dry leaves and bone
Alive to wolf law
A link in the pack.

I am wolf, not boy nor girl,
Not clothed nor upright.
My feet and hands are pads
From loping with wolves.

I smell as wolf smells,
I hunt as wolf kills.
I bite and claw.
Bones are my gnawing.

I know holes to hide in.
The call of owl and nightbird
Alert my ears, and my caution.
The air speaks to me.

My voice is wolf howl
My scars are huntplay

My eyes see as a wolf sees.
I am not other than wolf.

You may kill wolf and cub,
Bind me in net and rope.
I am wolf without shape or fur
But I know what a wolf knows.

I cannot smell your death
As I can my own
I cannot balance on legs:
Acrawl my back is strong.

Chain me. Beat me. Stretch me.
I am wolf—wild—uncruel.
Tame me and I will close
My eyes and feel your fear.

My head knows only wolf knowing
My blood pumps at wolf pace,
My pictures are den and forest,
Food and river, fang and fur.

I know wolf: I am wolf.
Even when I see other sights
And know other sounds
I belong to those who raised me.

Should I come to you
And lay my neck bare
For chain and fetters
How would you tether me?

I have been hunted

In the shadow of rock on cold sand
We ball in sleep. A waking sleep
Each pore and hair alert in a sleep
That charges muscle and heart.
My skin is sensor.
My thighs flex in sleep
I know where the ant moves.

59

Around us the rock is blade
In their shadow is shield.
A safe, warm, sour smell
Of sleep is everywhere.

A noise began.
A grain of other sound.
There was no mark
For it. It trembled the sand.

There is no diagonal hoof dance
For measuring the distance
The noise began.

It could be from before life begins
Or from where death is.

It drives sleep out.
That high clattering whir
Pumps blood into muscles
And drives sleep out.
A long hiss rakes the desert.

The night scent filled with a sweet sickness.
The herd alarmed. Stamped, circled deeper
Among the black doors of rock.

We fret and circle in rock shelter.
The noise and smell cast more fear
Than any knew how to rhythm—
How to stamp out.
We dither in shadow.

Sands heave towards us.
Dunes rise and come at us.
We close our heads in terror
And shiver into rock cracks.
The air noise nails us.

The wall is screaming sand
Passes swept on
Away from the snagging rock
Away from the herd.

Sand settles.
The sweet-sour smell crusts us
A wind teases scrub
Our heads ease in quiet.
We move.

Two females dropped dead fawn
Now lick them dry.

I close my body against
Tingling flanks.
My eyes are wet
My tongue like bone.

Sun torched rock shelter
We ringed around
And moved out
To the dew crops.

Dialogue

There is meaning in sand, and in rock,
In the way lizards run, in rat holes, in bone.

There is meaning in a clump of thorn, in root,
In quivering skin, in a stamped hoof.

A muzzle jerked over the neck marks distance
Close enough to bound, close enough to sniff.

There is meaning in flick of ears, roll of eyes,
In the shape of dune, in tongue lick.

There is meaning in tail whip, and in sun,
In the way dew falls, and in thorn strike.

A crossed dance of four hoofs tells of things
Beyond sight, beyond grasp of ear or eye.

There is meaning in sleep, in a new fawn,
In the stiff legs and dry skin of an old nurse.

There is meaning in a wound, and in blue clay,
In the horn's clash and the shielding circle.

There is meaning in what moves or does not,
In what is seen, and what is not.

Stranger

At a waterhole I lean over the still water
And see the sun.

I put my tongue to the water and a tongue
Licks at mine.

It tastes of water. I see a mane of black hair
And a sniffing nose.

It moves as I move. I call to it but there
Is no call back.

I nod and jerk my head, it does the same:
Moves as I do.

I put out my hand to catch it; it breaks.
My hand is wet.

Old nurse

Quivering ceased.
Under white sun
She falls onto white sand.
Her breath is fast
Barely escapes her open mouth.

She is on her right side.
Fragile legs straighten
And are frozen.
Her flanks are still
Her nose dry.

Flies cloud in
And cover her eyes
And search her mouth
For breath.
The black shroud
Covers her.

Beyond sight
Desert dogs whine
Sniff the air
And move towards her.

From all the hot sand
Creatures begin their part
In her death.

We move away
Away from that bundle
Quivering now with life
Not its own.

Later when we return
Over this white sand,
In white sun, the place
Will roll white bones
At our feet.
The old nurse is sand.

I move into line
My senses a chain
In this desert.

Boy of Aveyron

Alone. A lone child
There is no other.
No hand to clasp
No comfort to seek
From skin warmth
From mingled breath.
I know no other.

No parent. No kin
To learn, to chatter,
To romp or to eat with.
Each sense is hooked
On the mouth of living:
Without tear or laughter
Without heat or cold.

A hollow grey beech root
Clams this curling me,
Feeds with three edged nuts
Covers with blade leaves.
The tumble I know is green
And blue and sparkled black
Growing and falling—green alone.

I grasp a hem of oak.
Soothe me fern, tear me bracken.
Brook slap is running and still
Nothing I see—answers.
The pictures my eyes break
While I sleep bound
From trap, from fang, from claw.

Alone. A lone child.
That which I am
Is the limit circle
Of my root search,
Food ring, pool lap,
Is the path from beech
To bone and back to me—alone.

I know no other,
Hear no noise beyond those
At Aveyron. Loneness.
Where I am is me
That shields and grows me
Drawn from me open in me.

My muscle and sinew dance
To sounds that carry
Into these quiet ears.
I run, I hide, I burrow,
I climb into the noise

Carried by my whirled head
Which map hollow root and cave.

I know no hand to hold
No voice to soothe or chastise.
I know no extremes
Because I am. I am...
Alone—absorbed by all that is
Outside me. I know no one.
I am alone. Aveyron. A lone.

Whose silence, Aveyron?

My ear will answer
To forest, valley and hill.
Ice and sun brother me, rain
Silvers me.
When kniferock or bramble bleed me
I finger thin
Bright blood until the thunder
In my heart is dull.

I have never trapped light
Between thumb and forefinger.
My voice is culled
From screech-owl and fox.
At night in a hole I wake haunted
When wolf or wild dog
Hold me fawn-frozen.
Night pins me.

My blood is a fire tempered
Along my towering spine.
My fingers crackle
Ten restless daggers
That follow green eyes and scan
For long teeth.
No vowels tunnel this wordless mouth,
No gesture props me.

I am deaf in the household
Blind to a mirror

Mute for the witness.
From the city of my bones
I am caller and called.
I am one plane of eye and mouth
And limb.
All else is meaningless.

The wild boy is taught

Each day my eyes renew
From a dry oak hollow
Not pitched over a city howl.
A blind yesterday is lax
Only this morning begins at dawn.

I am trapped. I am named.
Yesterday and tomorrow assail me.
The door and wall and window,
The bed, table, plate, and my garb
Confuse and burden me.

They come to me with keys
In their voice, with chains
For hands, with thorn in their eyes.
They sound me a name....
O I cannot recall my forest.

For me today is what I see,
Potatoes, nuts, water, feed me.
I sway half asleep in a corner
I can see the leaves fall
From a tall tree but not on me.

One sound is name: that name
Holds me from the wind and grass.
The walls and this door block
All I know from what I see.
I do not know how to wake.

Their tongues and lips tire me,
Their hands and fingers gabble
To fix and grasp my eyes and break

Rain and river from the silence
Of the mirror I know.

They name me with their hands
Their tongues lock my name to my ear
Today is the wall I leap.
They close my circle and wring
Tears from me I cannot shed.

Girl of Songi becomes a nun

I lived in shadow between leaf and tree,
In a forest without a word or song,
On the live sinew between blood and bone.

I was one with the oak, and with the shade,
I was clad darkly with the thicket.
My mouth cracked walnut before rosary.

My eyes were all of my divinity
And soul, coupling me to known wildness.
I lived on a hilltop and by the moon.

I have lived without parable or sin
But here in this bricked cloister I am
Unable to part from everything.

On my knees in this still garden I watch
As shockwaves of air bound and fall
Between my lips and my prayer.

I watch the ant and the mayfly explode
Yet I know no tear for them.
I am a ring of prayer without end.

Today I wed the hand that separates
Tree and cross, that joins blood to crown,
While I stumble between the word and god.

CIRCLES

The name of the village is on maps
Of South Devon; it will have no name
Because it is childhood territory.

A boy's fantasy blurs the picture
Splinters home, armies, and blood-letting
As each memory furnishes what it recalls.

White clothes, white book, white rosary
Tarnished by convent ink flicked
From a girl's pigtail dipped in inkwell

Turned red. Later those blots
On shirt, on trousers, on buckskin shoes
Were stains from Plymouth blitz.

The marks drilled through cloth and skin
Into bone marrow and brain cell
Until confession was awash with blood.

No absolution could erase
Every schoolday. Holy days were violent
With demolition and desertion.

At school Latin verbs were declined
As hands assembled a Lewis gun,
And ink on the fingers dripped red.

There was a playground of tank and jeep,
Compounds to raid, and uniforms to fit
Over thin limbs in lonely homes.

The village street was a highway
To invasion littered with waste
Of 'C' rations and discarded packs.

Ally and enemy filled the trucks.
Swallow and spitfire vied for air
While children turned flint inside.

Behind the main street a Square
Was haunt for evacuee and village boy.
We fought over our territory.

Between slaughterhouse and wheelwright
A conflict as bitter as Europe's flared—
Inches and imagination grabbed power.

Our homes were empty of dominion,
Of compassion, even love or company.
Instead we invented our childhood.

Codes snarled language. We squirrelled
Catapult, club, airgun. Evasion our game.
The cry was: never tell, never tell.

Through the village a convoy
Of trooptrucks wheeled a khaki horde
And into the Square cattle carriers

Unloaded bullocks for butchering,
The double slaughter doors wide open
Almost a stage set for an act.

Chains hung still and gleaming
The gutters were scrubbed clean
Axe and cleaver were silver sharp.

Three thousand landingcraft bristled
Towards beaches at Utah and Omaha
And fell to Sword, Juno, and Gold.

Overhead Typhoons rattled summer,
Petrol and diesel closed out the rose,
Bullets took the air of hiving bees.

We village boys coralled the cattle,
We knew this short trail.
Evacuees stayed behind the valley wall.

After hoofskidding from a truck
Bullocks must be quieted, soothed,
And calmed—no quivering flesh.

Just keep them moving and make
Deep, soft calls. Round and around
Until the aproned foreman beckoned.

Then herd them between the fences
Two by two along the platform
Where from a cable the humanekiller

Swung to the slaughterman's hand.
Beside him an axeman waits
To stove the skull, hitch hooves to chain.

We were skilled at prodding cattle
Through that double run and we barely
Noticed the gutter of blood.

Nor the blood rain that splattered
Our oversized military shirts,
Nor the double thud of gun and bomb.

We children would calm the bullocks
In the Square and lead them to slaughter
For sixpence and the longest horns.

At the summer beach a bike ride away
Files of soldiers packed landingcraft
Quiet but for scrape of boot and stifled cough.

We cycled our racing Armstrongs
To watch the concourse from the cliff.
We lay flat on the grass and counted

Until counting gave out and the quake
Of tanks tickled our bellies.
We never saw the departure.

The war rolled through and flew over.
We heard and saw it outside our pitched
Games—all one way to the coast

Then the return. Convoys both ways.
Dead. Wounded. Prisoners inland:
More quick men towards the sea.

We continued to work cattle for the gun
And were rewarded. Freely we gleaned
Souvenirs to daub our culled uniforms

Collected from the litter on the beach
And from prisoners-of-war and 'G.I.s'.
We sesamied the cave of war.

I watched victory night from a window
At the front of the house. Saw no-one
And celebrated nothing. There was nothing I knew.

The calendar span and Europe expired.
Parents returned and were estranged
To us, to home, and to themselves.

Anger was pent and chained as hooves
Of the cattle I'd watched hanging
In the slaughterhouse and in dream.

Waking was violent with loneness,
Love seemed to leak away from gutters
Of blood I could smell in sleep.

There was no surrender, no return.
I left the village to renew itself
While I gathered pieces of me

For a jigsaw which had no picture
Just words that dropped from my lips
As water off oilskin. Warmth scorched my heart.

Later I took to trees and rivers
For company. The grass was constant
And the sky, and these I made mine.

Among streets and books I searched.
I looked for shape in museums
And unreeled dream in Odeons.

But there was nothing until Zennor
Cliffs dragged out a song for mermaid
And her reply beguiled me.

A stubborn hook struck
And barbed in to my head and heart
Raising a line from Cove Cottage

To the war I would not fight.
Deliberate tribunals farced
My angry dreaming and judged

A just war was uniform for me.
But I was raw with the cattle
And from tallying landingcraft.

Three times I refused to move
Into Call-up line, into sullen line.
Magistrates passed sentence

And I heard the cell door clang
While keys echoed away on chains
As the circling continued.

I watched the grey-clad prisoners
Turn round and around a narrow path
As they exercised an hour

A day in the yard beneath
My window. I watched them
Herded, and caught the scuff

Of boots and drifting cough.
Locked away I sat and listened
Until pictures whirled and fused

Into so many taunting links
That all release was fettered
Within the limit of my skull.

For two months I scoured
Myself alone in a cell, sterile
Lockup, where the sound of my voice

Whipcracked beyond barred windows
Back to the scene in the Devon Square.
The boy grew. The boy grew.

Until down, down below dream
The sound and smell of village Square
And the circling cattle remained

As acceptance that chaos was crop
With season and pickings in childhood.
A door slammed that only love could key.

Gradually tumbler after tumbler
The lock unfastened and I stood
With a hand on the handle.

I found my free hand grasped
With love. And the need to love
Turned the child's splintered mirror.

Normandy now has no Mulberry Harbour.
Summer air is packaged with jets
And barbedwire rusted from the shore.

Memory held too long enlarges fear
And confuses itself in bitten anger.
I was ashamed of love: and carcasses.

The man returned and his mirror held.
I saw the familiar names on bakery,
Post Office, and sweetshop. The Square

Is as different as the date—and so am I
From that lank lad who drove his heart
Beside cattle and khaki trucks.

The pictures that had me bound
Fell away. Along the main street I merely
Ghosted the careering bike and recalled

The tennisball thrown to jam in spokes.
Today I walk through the Square
And slaughterhouse doors open to stripped pine.

I reminisced down Church Street
And thought I heard tapdancing and felt
The first kiss from Joyce by Runaway stile.

Houses we rampaged looked like snapshot,
There's no 'homing' to the postbox
The village is quiet about its day.

I drove from that Devon village
Left the sound of cattle skittering
From my skull to haunt the Square.

The prime boy was fantasy.
The war gone. The cattle dead.
Sixpence is no decimal for love.

THE YEAR'S MEASURE

May 12

Each day in my garden
beneath a young elm
I watch and wait
for the swallows.
From early leaves caterpillars
hang like a green curtain
on long threads.
I wait for the swallows
while apple and plum leaves
are invaded.

On May 12th they came,
the afternoon sun was warm.
As I moved to the buddleia
by the shed, a sharp blue wing
stitched under the lip of thatch
turned on a tip and stalled
onto an oak beam.

Into uncalendared summer
two swallows patrol and acrobat
above the garden.
They strafe our cats,
victory roll over the mower,
seam through the shed-door
to nest on an oak beam.

June 12

Rhododendrons, mauve and pink, in last bloom
flank Eling Wood. Young ferns uncurl.
Full oak and beech leaves shutter the sun.
The path is dry, grass crisp.
Heavy scent hangs in the air
I walk lightly not to disturb the bees.

From a sand track I pick an eggshaped stone
and throw it from hand to hand
as I pass deeper into the wood.

She is outlined in shade.

Two cuckoos fly
together from branches cuckooing
in slow flight.
I stand and watch.
At my feet a young hedgehog snuffles
through bramble and grass,
it stops by my boots.

I kneel and whisper her name.

The hedgehog creases its face
and dark eyes peer down dark nose.
We stay unmoving. The wood is quiet,
no bird seems to call.

She is weeping.

I shifted and the hedgehog
began to curl then relax and deliberately
scrape passed me leaving small marks,
like bramble scratches, on my boot
as it burrowed into the rhododendron.

Her tears burn.

July 12

I drove home through midnight
the road became my blindfold:
Gauges stare a green glow
and rain nailed the fabric roof.

The storm gathered

Wide tyres splattered through water
headlights picked at dark clumps
of foliage, a sky of leaves showered
coins of rain at my windscreen.

Thunder is pent in her heart

I slowed through the gears
knowing I had driven into her storm.
Five miles from home I stopped
to peer along the beams. Silence clammed.

Lightning split the night

Rain slowed its rhythm; and colour
filled a box of hedge and trees.
I stepped out on to the road
and leaned against my car

half pinned between headlights
and shadow. Moths gathered at bulbs
dusting glass with wingbeat.
I stayed in shadowed rain.

Her eyes are broken by tears

Out of pitched hedge from my left
a young dog fox loped
and stood for a moment in the light,
his red eyes turned to the car.

As he moved the beam lengthened.
Mat in dipped light the fox crossed
the road and broke out
of my blood's blindfold.

She has blown summer

I waited, shrugged off the rain
ducked into my seat,
dragged a belt across my chest
and geared myself for home.

The season of her heart closed.

August 12

High above my cottage
and over the beech wood
against fathomless backcloth
two hawks lazily combat
as they climb, stall, dive, turn
on summer thermals.

During this stone-hot day
my eyes are knots
that ache from watching. The sun burns me
as each antic
glimmers shock-talons I imagine
in the air grace I see.

I hear nothing. Wings beat a loud
silence I can almost hum.
Two hawks circle and cross,
divide then exchange
the air temple of each ritual.

Afternoon has no end,
while these hawks stoop the sky is full
of blood that drips
from their eyes and drop by drop crushes me
as it enters my skull.

August unwinds towards my winter.

September 12

They are gone.

The last time I saw them I was crouched on a boulder
overlooking a storming sea.

They ganged up and left.

All summer we shadowed one another.
Swallows raked the air
while I lugged my mower through the grass.

Much has moved with this September
it's as though the fullness of seed
burst more than simple ripeness.

Mist and top dew are so heavy
my head and eyes cannot contain them.
I can barely keep warm. Pinpricks shiver and mark
the atlas of my bones and trace flight
across heartbeat with spinning compass.

They ganged up and left.

And I cannot stay where I am even though
harvest mice move among logs stacked by fireside
and spiders lengthen their webs across
window and door. The air welcomes frost.

I wait as the moon scans the lane
printing gate and oak on the tarmac
blanked out by shadows
I half recognise. Hulks of memory
skitter behind my eyes.
There was a time when love was in
my going out and returning. Does it matter
where I am as this September
bursts my nostrils with its melancholy?

Between flight and dance there is destiny
ending and beginning on swallows' wings.

Underfoot the fallen fruit is crushed
and rots on the grass.

Through heavy rain I notice that leaves
begin to patch the boughs
then fall.

October 12

Two-faced October
is passing with its summer ghosts
harnessed to dark months of autumn
riding every falling fruit.

This October ripped trees clean
and has blown the gaff on truth.
The storm outside my cottage echoes
a turmoil in my heart's blood.

Two-faced October has a sharp edge
of promise outlining winter's finery.

October salted summer wounds
and turned my blood cold
twisting each nerve end like a leaf
about to be unhinged from a bough.

And I benight myself
with nightmare that is myth
for the hurt of October.

Among windfalls and fallen leaves
the serpent has a familiar face.
His broken tongue is edged blue and red
and secret tenderness poisoned me
from Spring and Summer to melancholy October.

My heart is storm: my nightmare flares.
October is two-faced and both torment me.

Yet I must love
and see the ghost and nightmare fade
into iron November
so that seeds of love are held
for renewal as seasons unfold.
October is our death and our renewal.

I watch the litter bunch in corners
against hedge and wall. I see grass grow pale
then with eyes of October I see love
tempered anew in a mirror reflecting
the Janus face of this Ortober.

November 12

The year has spun knots
tighter and tighter each hour
that deepens to winter.

I cannot recall summer
but see her mask smile,
fingers touch without warmth.

From my tangled heart
a blood tear breaks
with coldness I cannot bear.

Meaningless words revolve
so fast I do not know
what is from what is not.

Now words are hollow.
Love I seek is sleeping
as November closes.

My laugh is sharp, my touch
scars, knife tender,
cutting all waking, all sleep.

The turn of November
does not herald joy
as its grip distances us.

So I turn to flame
to burn my lips
and seal our wasting love.

December 12

Pain bit, despair cried holly and ivy
and from a stable the birth sang out.
In my eyes grotesque shade of love
played on the walls, on the floor,
on my face mirrored and blank.

Stars led, gifts held mystery,
animals stood about dumb.
The pain around us bled—lapis lazuli.
As I reached out to touch her
my love gushed in floods that could drown
all love from birth to this December.

There was no control, no stopping events.
Each denial, each timber, each beast
pitilessly cast its shadow.

She held her breath against the onslaught:
And the agony, etching her eyes,
alone crossed nightmare with nightmare.

Then she was gone. The year closed.
I stayed in an emptiness of straw
eating at fallings of love so brittle they tore
my lips and cut at the core of me.
And she swam through her tears drowning,
drowning as every tear drove the flood.

January 12

We turned to each other and held quiet.
Winter claimed darkness. Rain fell
until the earth was awash and our eyes
could meet without blinding. Without hurt.

Days of January laboured with hours
poised on a pinhead. The angels fell off
leaving snowdrops and our wanting to correct
the balance that we had upset.

Night and day a new year settled
healing our wounds as our blood slowed
so hand could clasp hand, and lips meet:
silence was fuel, and food, and balm.

Crocuses taunt grass while January
tilts to Spring. Lost months
slide away and the silence holds
our hearts as the frost gives way.

February 12

In bloom a white rose haunts me.
There was a heartstop which no surgeon
could restart, nothing transplant.

Winter hours sealed pain as heart
upon heart broke and ghosts of summer
loomed in distorting eyeflame

of confused love. A white rose
defies frost and trumpets at Spring
as our pulsebeats reclaim us.

Autumn and winter had filled
with ember and ash. February
rises from midwinter fires.

Daffodils coin gold for Spring
while we breathe shallow not to catch
ash afire. Instead our charred

memories melt into sleep
at midnight, into passing winter
which closes last year's diary.

March 12

A whisper turns to song,
wind partners flower and bud.
The air is warm and I feel
her fingers move to mine.

A bramble-edged track
leads to and from our hearth.
Nettles are skin hungry
and net-over fresh scrapes

where pheasants nest.
A long Dale field ropes
shadow-boxing hares full
of dreams of summer grass.

Our willow bobs silver tails
at retreating discontent.
Birds bicker for inch of hedge,
soil asthmas with rain.

85

Our silence is whispering;
blood runs against dark days
that fractured our eyes.
We wait. Her tongue touches mine.

We watch. Silence bridles.
Tension burrs at neck and shoulder,
love and renewal awake,
voice and eye mount Spring.

April 12

Between barely green boughs
a hawk straightened thoughtless
towards his acre of sky.

A wind whipped branch
tripped his wing so he dropped
onto the narrow path
ahead of me.

I stood. The hawk
swayed dusting his wings
glaring around to threaten
mud and root and stone.

A bunch of anger
he haunched on hook talons
then drove his beak
at the clumsy earth.

Preening his feathers
he flexed his wings
and rose through hedgetrees
to bolt over Eling fields.

GROTESQUE TOURNAMENT

Grotesque Tournament

The princess arms him with a lance
then she places a crest on his helmet,
it is blue and gold—a token he will
carry as he defends her honour
in her fight.   He is proud.

His warhorse is a unicorn.
His squire, a monkey, cavorts at the bridle.
She sews a gold symbol on blue trappings;
an armour, she says, nothing can penetrate.
He holds aloft a lance.

Then in rides the challenger,
a bull on the back of a goat.
Gauntlet and insult are exchanged.
On the bull's shoulder a vulture cackles.
The unicorn and rider shiver.

A pageant arrives to referee the joust,
first a fox trailing a scarlet cape from its neck
is led in by a gorilla on a stag
outflanked by a rabbit and a hare
dancing flag dances.

Around the arena thumps a wildman
horns on his head and Ash in his hands.
A wildwoman rides in on the back of a griffin,
she waves effigies of men and women.
The winter trees are black with rooks.

Banners in red and gold and blue stream
from poles that are brandished by bears.
A trumpet heralds the contest.
From one side of the field he spurs the unicorn,
from the other the bull snorts at the goat.

Dead centre on a high raised dais
the princess sits with her hands on her lap,
the back of her right hand in the palm of her left.
She has an overview of the contest
and of the whole grotesque tournament.

The Imperfect Knight

I am a knight with a name in the air,
with arms that bear image of eagle
and comet, whose motto is cold as steel.

My weapons are obscure as moondust,
my lands are on the horizon of my skull.
In the palm of my hand I seek the grail.

I am of the order whose silence breathes
witchcraft unblemished in its own quiet.
My eyes are space, empty within my helmet.

I am the champion who combats in green mist
but cannot enter into tower or court
without feeling closed walls break me.

I am of the sash whose place is left vacant
at the last table, whose couch is unslept-on
whose voice is snapped off by the receiver.

I am the shadow at the corner of the eye
and the distorted word. I cannot ask
a question because the answer barbs too deep.

I am the knight everyone knows in passing
and keeps at a distance; too close I am blurred
because I am everyone bewitched by the mirror.

Gothic Dream

This cast is in a heraldic dream.
When you wake you will remember
Details distinct in tone and colour
And the meaning will be clear.

An epic chronicled on a sheet
So huge it takes the whole night
To contain it, and a godshead
To direct its jigsaw elements.

There is no frame, no border,
Everything rotates and is reeled
In the bedtossed hours or seconds
Of the pictured, sleeping symbols.

From crafted pen and eye the page
Is filled until it spills out
Into you to become alive
And wilful deep in your head.

Somewhere almost out of sight
And hovering above a bluescaled
Lion, a dragon is eating a red painted
Child. Night is filled with angels.

In the right eye under a gold orb
A radiant face is crowned by
Seraphim as light and colourful
As beads on an infanta's hair.

In the left over bed and roof
A slither of silver sucks in heads
Whose halos make a chain that trails
And spirals through everything.

Two beaked lions panache their manes
Into a storm sky, and they growl
At a raging sea until their breath
Makes a tornado spin out of your dream.

Far below on a stylish shore peacocks
Turn their backs on the falcon,
Two hounds sniff at grazing deer,
Crane and swift dance heraldry.

The room is quiet, through an open
Window a breeze touches your shoulder
And the panorama dissolves
Through a crack in the floor.

The alarm keys into your dream
And the cast shed their roles
To become angles in the geometry
Of your room and measure of waking.

The Last Show

Near midnight the television
screen flickered and the colour
rolled up like a blind leaving
a mat grey glass with its reptile
eye shutting out the picture.

But behind the blank screen
there is a turn in the path
where icons swirl on a page
of circles, each circle a story
within itself.

The princess sees an otter with a fish
in its mouth, the fish had three tails.
Also watching the otter are two cats,
and four mice nibbling a wafer.
The story foretold itself.

A purple eagle beats eight wings
against a sharp horned, ox-faced lion.
Seven white doves circle a gold goose
while acid green moths put out
the candle that burns once a night
until the chalice is drained.
Then colour returns to the screen
leaving the outside banal
and the inside empty.

The girl fingers the remote control.
She stretches out and places
her left hand on her right shoulder
and her right hand on her left shoulder.
This way she will sleep; and dream
of a snake eating a snake eating a snake.

Kermis

A jester cavorts in front of the infanta.
The bells on his green pointed shoes are mute.
On his blue cone hat a bell clatters
to the rhythm of his shaking head
but he cannot make the infanta smile.
Her dream has ridden away over the forest
on the back of a winged horse.
The dream has left a chain of pearls
across the night and one full shell that hangs
from a backdrop as a token of her dream.

The jester has lost his nerve.
If he doesn't amuse her he will forfeit
all his life is worth.
The infanta thinks of nothing but her loss—
tapestries are drained of texture
and the lights dim as the jester stumbles
and drops his stick. He can no longer jest.
He is afraid because he sees a tear of ambergris
in her left eye and in her right a tear of tar.
The folk urge the infanta to open the carnival.

The Gift

A babyfaced serpent
twines four times
round the branches of a tree.
Three stags and a cow
stand or sit
by a clear river.
Two white rabbits sleep
while a squirrel
and a mouse
eat fallen fruit.
From a fir tree
a hawk adorns the sky.

Leaning against
a tree Eve holds
a heartshaped

fruit in her right
hand and in her
left a gold ring.
Near Eve's knee
a seahorse jogs in
dark water only it can see.
Adam's right hand
is held out
to receive a gift.
Behind him two men
look content their
arms are folded
and legs crossed
down to cloven hoofs.

The babyfaced serpent
winks over Eve's
shoulder at a girl
who at another
time pulls a shower
curtain along its
goldringed rail as
she begins to
prepare for a party
given by the gardener.
She has apples
gift-wrapped for him.

Trial by Love

From a window in a castle tower
the princess lowers a basket
large enough for a lover to hop in
and be winched up to her chamber.

Below in the slime-thick moat
creatures with steel incisors
are ravenous, their yellow eyes
taste the dropping basket.

The lover is silly with lust,
he floats on an ark of gossamer

to catch the lift. The basket sways
halfway across the moat—inviting.

He calls to the princess for help.
She cannot bear to watch so turns away.
He drops his sword and dagger
to lighten himself as much as possible.

He high steps for the leap. Up he soars.
She has gone into her room.
His hand reaches for the basket, but misses.
The princess hears the snapping teeth.

She sighs as she rewinds the winch.
In the distance another lover
on a white horse canters to the castle.
In the slime the creatures wait.

Play Blues

One day the princess just took off.
She'd had enough of jousts
and carousing, she'd heard all the jokes,
seen tumblers, plate-spinners, bear baits.

The prince drank too much with his friends
who broke precious jars and tore dresses
off her maidens. The prince became coarse
and he didn't try to understand her.

Instead he'd outline a far campaign,
go over old victories and boast wildly.
It was too much for the princess
so she untied her golden hair and left.

The prince was distraught, he called for
his minstrels and commanded them
to compose dirges and bitter laments
for the loss of his own true love.

As the lutes droned and pipes whined
the minstrels rhymed for the love

of the dove that strove to find the grove
where the princess had moved to reprove

the prince who wept as he listened
to ballad after goldseeking ballad
until one minstrel turned his lute
around and drummed out a blues.

The prince then tore strips off a red skirt
and pinned a cross on his chest, he knew
he must lead a crusade over the sands
and take the blues to Jerusalem.

Standard Doodle

A rage of undrawn figures curl
down the margin of the page until a file
of falcon, phoenix, priest and pariah
waylay a procession of pilgrims
whose stories wail in unborn ears unable
to shut out the ceaseless chatter.

The page flaps as if six demented wings
thrashed the air, and a vacant eye
reads names it could not, dare not, name.
Falcon and phoenix halt all traffic.
Priest and pariah wait at cathedral steps
while a purple dust falls over them.

At a precinct a standardbearer
leads the pariah who leads the priest
to where a neon phoenix blazes
and a falcon revolves in a window.
It is there pilgrims consume them while
Sirens loop a melodic madness.

Absorbed at his drawingboard a boy
stabs felt tip rainbows on the page
as he doodles shield and axe and cross
beside a crude castle where falcon preys,
phoenix holds its fire,
and stick pilgrims tumble down a sign of pax.

NEW AND UNCOLLECTED POEMS

The Prize

I listen to him build paper dominions
and spell pages with alchemic dream.

In my hand the iron smoothes a blouse I
will wear when the music and dance begin.

In his room he beats bounds with a head as
full of compass and signpost as mappa mundi.

I weed the garden to soothe the harp
that grows in me bursting with endless song.

The words grow, and song fashions its tune
there is music but the dance is elsewhere.

At table our voices are quiet then strident,
rise and fall reaching for each other without rest.

His hand settles on the plate but he is held
by the picture in his head, by the siren

which has no response to the song vibrating
under my tongue. I see the blouse I ironed.

It is like a habit, a promise I must keep.
I know there will be dance. I will dance.

He mouths at a tune. I see his eyes
disguise their pain as he breathes towards me.

He moves with a whole domain on his back
which he brings to me like a colossal prize.

I cannot look. The song I sing grows,
jigs, kicks its heels. I will not take his prize.

It's too heavy and burdensome for my dance,
instead I reach away to take up my blouse.

Daughters

Sometimes it is so dark in my head
that the chatter falls like rock
against the back of my eyes.

I sit looking at the fire but feel
no warmth nor do I see anything
on the crowded mantlepiece.

The clock spins. Invitations curl
with a cruel sneer. Endlessly
I turn the ring round my finger.

The child is asleep. I hear her cot
move and hold my breath so's not
to wake her. I ache for sleep.

Around me the room is quiet
but the traffic and stamping inside
is so busy I'm afraid to rest my arms.

Somewhere distant or long ago
I recall this room festive
and fragrant. A kitten played.

Everything has changed—voice
to clarion, quiet to bond,
warmth and time to loneliness.

I raise a hand and see rash
marks on the palm, and broken nails.
Even the ring is tarnished.

She is asleep and dreams dreams
I dreamed. Her white dress is cotton,
hair ribbon green, her shoes red.

I am dreaming, awake, asleep;
or somewhere between all three
as I sit listening for my breath.

My chest moves but it is with her

breath. I'm alert to her waking
afraid of her exploding tears.

They crush me with demands
I have not will enough to give
nor gift enough to join.

She tore me between love and dream,
between her desire and mine. I whisper
my name which is hers. Hers. Hers.

From the Front

He returned from war
and she cried.

He was unmarked outside
but in his head vivid clouds flared.

She held his shoulders,
cut the wood, dug the garden,
cooked their food, cleaned the house
and fed him with salves.

Daylight gave him ease in open fields:
woods were too dense, too dark.
Traffic glazed his eyes. Houses and shops
trapped a nerve in his ears and
drove him into his skull's blackhole.

She read their old letters
to him. He listened but the din of her
tears and the red film behind his eyes
scrambled the words.
Shut out that love.

She watched him drum
his fingers on his knees, watched his muscles
stiffen and quiver. She took him to bed and held
him as night clanged alarms
along his sinews.
And she cried.

He walked along the lane
close to the hedge. A car exhaust
or pheasant burst would send him
headlong and flat into the undergrowth.

She bought him brandy
and more tobacco. She made him thick
earmuffs to counter noise.
She bunkered the house
and foxholed their letters from his war.
She held her husband—not the soldier.
She held herself and them
in a vice of love.

Pictures in his head remained
mud splattered and framed by unendurable
flesh and bone.
A dog whistle or sharp
voice held him rigid, eyes straight, shoulders
eager, his hoe at ready sloped from left to right.
She ran to him
and stood behind his shoulders whispering
until the hoe lowered and he slumped forward
holding himself up by the shaft.

She cried.
The doctor prescribed Valium,
said her husband should be in a Home
looked after by trained people.
Her training was love,
her strength her love, her skill love.
She cried.

Month by month she forged her sinew
to his and linked each move she made to him.
He screamed in the night and fought
the day.
There was not a mark
on him yet his head raged and his blood
froze and burst the seeping scars.

She cried.
There was not a mark on her
except furrows down her cheeks, on her
forehead, around her eyes.

In her head the sound
of him was like marching. She choked as
his footfalls drummed their path. She span
black circles in her head as he climbed
the stairs.

Her head went
to war and woke each morning wounded.
Her head raged and her blood froze....

He cried.

Sonnet

to my great grandmother

Over her bed a holy water font
fine crafted in metal: red, green, and gold.
The room was sombre since she didn't want
drapes open, preferring shadow and cold.
She believed that in heaven there'd be young
men on white horses who would escort her
through valleys to a shore where mermen sung
the ballads she knew. Winter she would stir
fingers in the font, cross herself then suck
the liquid dry. Once she told me to taste
my fingers after cross, she said for luck.
I was not to let a sup go to waste.
I gagged as the warm needle tang kissed me
which I grew to know as Irish whiskey.

Sonnet

to my grandmother

She sat rock solid at the round table
a huge arm on the dresser plucking cups
like apples. Not stirring she was able
to command three generations, their ups
and downs soothed or frozen by Irish blue
eyes and serrated brogue. Rules were stone cast,
she was right and that was that, we all knew
first in was awarded the cherry, last
an icy word. Her kitchen was centre
of Christendom, food but an irksome chore
beyond concern. Talk, song, and gin lent her
power of the moon, we a tide to her shore.
All other rooms were exile, shells to hold
to an ear where her laughter sounded cold.

Sonnet

to my aunt Monica

She drove an ambulance through London Blitz
told tales of riding craters as though they
were sea surge. Such a legend retains its
memory with her laugh, almost a bray.
She fitted a blue lightbulb in a skull
to spook and liven the lavatory.
In the hall a gilt frame featured a dull
banana so old she made a story
of grandad bringing it from Africa
fighting off Fuzziwuzzi with one hand.
Her fun was complete: none comes after her.
Mo's somewhere making palaces of sand.
From London, Devon, or Fisherman's Wharf
here's another lady death cannot dwarf.

Sonnet

to my aunt Olga

Cocktails, ebony cigarette holder,
bobbed, lobe-level hair, reddest lips in town,
a fur slung carefully on her shoulder,
measured pleasure that never let her down;
this aunt was too much for a Devon boy,
too, too much even when later she took
me in hand she said, to let me enjoy
dimlit Chelsea nightclubs where I should look
and learn while smooth music bounced from the walls
where enough fruit-stacked booze would break the bank.
Her boyfriends had slicked hair and whipped drawls,
addressed each other by their demob rank.
Olga your time-warp style was a blessing
no act of nostalgia nor regressing.

From **The Company**

There was an afternoon when I heard him
slow the car into the garage. He'd call me
to strap on pads, put on green rubber-spiked
gloves, step in front of the stumps
to practise strokes while he bowled.
That summer has lasted as long as I remember.

He left for war. I grew and warred myself
from child to boy. The boy was moulded
by the boy's own hand and the aimless
fist of Europe's conflict.

I grew and argued. Grew away from the father
who flew among bullets and photographed
battle and destruction. Then he returned home
a different man, a man I'd grown out of.

He died in so many flames, pitched
from cockpit and couch into fires
(real and in dream) I pulled him from
but could not douse in him or me.

When the time for tears arose
there were not enough to moisten my cheek.
I had cried too long, too long alone.
I was not afraid but I was angry
and I'd see stars fall out of the sky
blossom into parachute to flame again
and candle into the earth. (I do not like
fireworks, they are full of memory.)

The nets he gave me closed in and I fought
to free the trap. Before he died I found
hill and cliff were high enough for breath.
I looked down, down into the valley village
then walked away.

He stayed in that blue uniform with hard
gold rings that hurt my neck like a collar.
He stayed as a shadow at the end of the pitch
propelling a red ball at me—for his or my
practise—we never lived to know.

How do I call you father when I did not learn
the language you brought home on leave,
never had the days to tell you
what I had really felt or made?
Your slipstream hours were too full and fast
for words to settle or silence to smother fire.

My first son, born where Magna Carta
was signed, arrived jaundiced
with spiked black hair. He was in a hurry
couldn't wait to gasp a lungful of air
and yell down confining walls.

He taught me fatherhood when his three
year hand led me to see a molehill
he'd constructed beside the mole's hill.
Home from school he'd rattle the gossip
tapping a ball from foot to foot.

End of term he'd be reluctant to show
his report with its 'Could do better

if he concentrated'. An echo etched
deep in me. Or '...he is a dreamer
who must wake up'. My response was
fatherly. But then to see him run
Eling Woods and gangle over fields
as he grew taller than me I asked,
Why?

His answer is his growing and his care,
in his way with wood and metal, chisel
and saw, as he builds his dream
in three dimensional stand which replies:
There is no dream that cannot be real.

My second son arrived as bluebells tolled,
he was quiet and would lie and watch
apple leaves from morning to dusk.

He led me into his dream as we slept
head to head one winter afternoon
when he was three. He taught me his laugh
and the way he stilled everything he saw,
his eyes became the sap focus of beech,
or gate or sunset. Swallows would take
him for swallow, he became their flight.

Together both sons reared a father
who, slow to learn, drank their care
as a gift, as a seed from forever.
They grew separate yet inseparable.

Both build, construct, make each day
a landscape which begins in pieces
until the pieces sculpt their dreams.

To My Mother

She died at the year's turn
How many times
I cannot be sure.

Hers were all exits—
From round mountained table
To Devon, to Honduras....

She leaned on a spinning Ireland,
Gave a seismic smile,
And packed a picnic basket.

But she forgot how to return,
Instead she gathered homeless places.
And it rained all summer.

A china pig painted with clover
Idolled her everything
In grandmother's huge shadow.

The blue jewels on three fingers
Changed nothing—
She was shy of spun gold.

We stand now in winter rain
Outside ourselves
Recalling our names:

Recalling her name
Drummed in requiem response.
O Spring is a winter away.

The Wall, The Ants and The Green Woodpecker

I planned to repair my garden wall,
Lift blue boulders and blue-white flint
Then straighten the bank of earth
Before I replaced the pieces.

On the grass bank neat holes
Drilled by a green woodpecker
Guided the crowbar I thrust
Deep beneath a stubborn stone.

As I levered that stone free
I broke into chambers, collapsed
Tunnels and opened long dry galleries.
The ants teemed. I could almost hear them.

My wall was down. Galleries and tunnels
Fell. I watched ants in formation lift
Eggs in quick patterns. Organise.
My wall was in disarray.

Then the rain fell and the fine soil
Spoilt and the going was slippery.
Around me a pile of stone and flint
Mocked my unreasoned building.

Single stones await order.
I watch the ants move
Into the raw bank of earth.
I take each stone to build my wall.

It is built. The slate in place.
Somewhere nearby galleries and tunnels
Are alive with ants. From a fallen
Apple tree the green woodpecker looks down.

Abercynon

At the face of Abercynon the cutting screw
Chews out a bite 2 ft 3 inches deep by 153 ft long.

In the lampbeams the coalface shimmers
Black that holds in it a memory of sun and rain.

Short hydraulic props probe flat iron plates
Against torn scars. And behind the prop the roof falls.

Coal and slate-dust clams mouth and nose and pores
To conceal the low tunnel and blot out thought.

The black dust breaks lampbeams, seeps into eye socket
Rasps on the tongue and is sour bile in the throat.

The coalface screams. A stream of water splashes
On tungsten cutters ripping out the narrow seam.

Crouched with more than a thousand feet on his shoulder
The miner holds a prop handle, pushes and turns to move the prop.

The iron plate grinds into the gap left by the cutter
Metal and coal war while a man crouches between

Moving each prop down the cut-line, adjusting thin mesh
Between prop and roof; joining mesh plates with silver spring.

Abercynon gives up its coke coal foot by foot,
Ton by ton, to the bone and flesh of miners.

Each face is unthinkably sunk below layers of earth.
Black lives. Black silence punches the whistle out of a man.

Below

On the surface black has depth
It breathes lungsful of itself
And spreads outwards released
From weight and walled silence.

Deep in the districts of a mine
The air is hard as bone
And black as though eyes
Stared backwards in their sockets.

At full run the silence
Hooks into the mouth of sound
And bit by bit tears
Into the seam of the skull.

Shale-fall, voice, lampbeam,
Dustsoftened footstep, water,
Machinery, airshute, everything
Below is barrier black silence.

Her Song

Early swallows dither the evening heather
And a March gale bats them from the East.

I return to Lundy where summer long
I held the dream of your copper hair

And kept your epitaph, your lines
Of love in stone, as siren and beacon.

My first visit you gave me your name
Above the bridal lace foaming from the shore.

Trust kept the gap in time. Your lines
Sing and link words through other years.

You and I both fell. You onto calling rocks
And I into verb for moondust and spindrift.

The basking seals moan and seem to weep
From fractions of rock that fill our eyes.

Your children are the kittywake and tern
My sons have grown into their babes.

Ours is the proud paradise you haunt
With words to echo summer long.

No wind or seamist, no heartbreak
Can escape the drift of your copper hair.

Latitude and dateline have etched
The searoute from my wood to Lundy

While each day mirrors your blue eyes
And the sea rises from your sleeping breath.

Today is calm. On Western cliff your voice
Reclaims the spell between our years.

Swallows career a spring sky for the young
And proud to wed again on the spinning isle:

A cloud closes in. She is calling.
Tomorrow I sail with a fragment of her song.

Robert Stephen Hawker, 1804-1875

Dear God but this August is tempting.

I walk my rocks and see that even gannets are full.

Yet I know that ballooning mainsails burst as ships
pass this headland, leaving only ablebodied souls
surefoot on dry rigging.

I cannot step the wind as it rebounds from these cliffs
against the winter panic that chills deep in me.

Along a path by the church I watch
autumn approach, and count leaves
knowing each will fall.

Then I must again carry the basket to the bay
where every leaf is a broken seaman
pinned under Vicarage Rocks.

Limb by limb I shall sanctify sea morsels
while part by part of me
seeps into Cornish soil.

O fill me God with song that I might hail
the distance between me, cliffs, and the sea-dead.

Mirrored

The roots of tree in the air feed off cloud,
Birds swim through mud and nest in tunnels.

The sun climbs west and is fierce at midnight.
Moonbathing gives a silver tan and goosepimples.

Walking or running backwards is fastest,
Be careful not to trip facing forward.

Hair grows inwards and warms the brain,
Not eating chocolate and creamcakes makes you fat.

Speaking and singing is the quiet way.
A hug and a kiss is hateful. Weeping is happy.

A grain of sand is too heavy to weigh:
Gold coins make the best ducks and drakes.

Yes is no and no word is noisy and loud.
Watch carefully behind a blindfold.

Sow seeds in the sky and reap in Spring
Count stars at your feet and pick flowers from the air.

Walk on the river and sea and all water
Be careful not to stray out of depth on road or path.

Nothing is what it seems. Surely not this;
Go make nothing into castles and high dreams.

Jardin de Ville, Grenoble

It was the dead swallow
folded wings and snaketongued tail
on the sand path at the base
of a lime tree at the far side
of the jardin de ville at Grenoble
that make me link the red
streak of sunset on Alp snow
with rings of wine on white cafe table

with tiles on the town roofs
and the dribble of blood on my finger.

It was the dead swallow
folded tail and scythe-air wings
on the morning sand in morning sun
in the dark shade at my feet
in the black shadow I cast
that made me link the blood
from my finger with the split in sky
playground among the roofs and trees
left by that bunch of vibrant flier
aground at the root of lime

It was the dead swallow
the wine lime trees morning sun
vacant cafe tables black shadows
and mountains that made the river
at Grenoble somehow run me down
to the streak of blood on my finger
between swallow flight love unendured
folded wings battened from the sky
in a colossal feathered death
at my shadowed feet.

It was the dead swallow
reminded me of my cottage shed
where five of them drill the doorway
to raven the air all summer
it was the dead swallow
in the morning garden at Grenoble
made me flinch from hurt I felt
at my heart's tumble and cast
off a stop of blood in the white sand
as token to no flight and no return.

Cathedral Garden, Bourges

I sit on a bench under lime trees clipped
for symmetry and shade. Five minutes past three
the sun is hot on the lawn.

In faded blue a gardener besoms a gravel path,
a girl in sunblaze T-shirt, jeans, and sunhat
follows him with wheelbarrow and boards
to collect precise sweepings.

A half carafe of wine has settled.
The sun burns my arms where I've rolled my sleeves,
moist fingers slide on my pen as I record
this passing in a cathedral garden.

Ahead of me red and yellow wallflowers
shoulder maroon, gold and blue pansies
hedged in by a two inch privet border.
Full roses among green and mottled leaf
attend the afternoon sun.

It is May 14th
yet the trees are heavy with summer.
Three sparrows dust the shade of copper beech.

At the right hand corner of the garden
from where I sit are two green and yellow parasols
shading a couple silent in each other's company.

Outside the garden traffic hums as the sun
blankets harsh noise.
Instead I hear the swish
of besom, the clatter of white butterfly wings,
the silken metre of rosary from a whitegowned nun—

and behind me the cathedral sighs with confession.

They came at me in black

A nun's shadow across desks,
Black hulk with siren voice
And ruler to tap, tap, tap
A warning before a tardy knuckle
Is hit.

Then black suit and shirt with white
Slash at the throat and voice
That charmed, chained, and commanded
A catechism. Who made you? Why
Did god......

I was decked out as a white
Parrot groomed from shirt to shoes,
Rosary to book—candle
To burn before I was seven. Before
I was.

They still came at me in black.
Grandfather's double-breasted
Regimental suit clouded
Over me; with no blessing he threw me
To swim.

Grandmother a ballad
Draped in black. Unseen muscle
And ebony cane moved her,
While her brogue burrowed under
Her tongue.

Black hearse carried them all
Father, mother, holy ghost,
Into the earth out of my
Burnt heart. I took a black taxi to green
Woodland.

Greenham Perimeter

Touch it and the ice burns
touch it and the flames freeze
Unknot the weave until the cloth
Stretches in a handheld circle
Around the outer fence of Greenham.

Straw woven through wire sings.
Photographs pale a girl's voice.
Put up needle and dread in tents
Among debris of home on the roadside:
By the Kennet there are dragonflies.

Do not let breaking cloud brick-up
A wall which cannot be renewed.
Do not ask women to chant a child
For tomorrow in a ruin of wire
Where to touch is to blaze and freeze.

Too Far From Home

I look over a ricefield,
And across a river
Whose name I cannot know.

In the water a crane stands
In the shade of a slender
Silverbarked tree.

High in the tree
A ragged nest sways
Between two boughs.

Nothing moves in the sun
But I know the crane
Is watching me.

There is no date
To this day since
I am too far from home.

Lines From Korea

The straw and stone
Of my house
Moves with me
Everywhere I travel.

They are my bone and blood.

They are the spring
In my step.

The single straw
Is weightless.
The blue edge of flint
Is strong.

To grow a man must
Love his home.

Interpreters

The two of them spoke little English
(I have no Korean). They are small
About five foot, with lank dark hair,
Dignified, yet quick with their smiles.

They drove me through patched country
To a village folk theatre
In a mountain valley where we sat
On seats carved smooth from granite.

Traditional play—a nagging wife
Goads a woodsman to cheat a wood's god
Who exacts revenge funny and cruel.
The audience knows the story.

Music colours the tale as strings slide
And each flute sets the muslin landscape
Into my eyes and into tableau
Of play and theatre and mountain.

118

Later at the village teashop
The interpreters bought ginseng
And sesame cake which we ate
In the sun on the veranda.

Villagers about their work gaped.
The two men made me understand
It was rare for *round-eye* to visit
A remote village and be alone.

Most of their words I had to guess
Since English so snagged their tongues
It fell out askew. And for them
My name was hard as chewing stone.

Across from the teashop a man drew
On handmade mulberry paper.
He would name a child, house, anything.
He painted the symbols on a scroll.

The interpreters went to him
And asked for my name—a name they
Could speak. The three talked while I
Drank my tea and gazed back at them.

He took down a scroll and stroked
His brushed over the surface,
Green, black, brown and blue figures
—three separate birds and a river.

The interpreters carried it back to me
And bowed my Korean baptismal
As they gave me the name......
HA IK SU.

Homecoming

When I returned she was there
Luggage, books and houseplants;
Her heartbeat in the cottage.

I had journied through tropics
And through fractured dreams,
I had burnt out my shivering.

Sweat had replaced tears
Salt had scoured my throat
Scars were no longer angry.

During the flight over oceans
And India, mountains and Europe
I sang and felt new veins throb

Saw the Boeing's grey wings
Beat inches of curved sky
And vapour the miles between us.

Her gentle hand recharged
The familiar. A question
Held in her eyes, on her lips.

We said nothing; stood together
Mingled our embrace and let
Silence voice our homecoming.

Seven Song

I watched my shadow grow
Until it shut out the stars and moon
And blacked the leaves
On seven summer trees.

I felt my shadow love
Until it failed to breathe beyond rooms
And wander towards
The seven mysteries.

120

I made my shadow hate
Until it backed into my skull
And drove out colour except
The seven tones of black.

I set my shadow free
Until it found moon-leaves in the stars
And bitter grown fruit
On seven summer trees.

Spindrift

You know where I go
You know where I've been.

Hold my hand, take my tears
Nothing here is for your ears.

I'm going where spindrift drives,
Breaking laughter from your eyes.

Leave me slate. Leave me iron.
Here's a love that I rely on.

From spring grass, from this quay
I'll drink my glass of malt whiskey.

Dream Garden

I dream and feel the summer crawl
Within the limit of my eye
As petals from a high rose fall
And leaves of oak shut out the sky.

I love the wild and clinging weed
That thrives among my cottage grass
No blade shall cut its curling need
To bind my dreams before they pass.

The mountains of this garden cease
Where oceans break upon the path:
The gate sighs on a hinge of grief
While burning logs glow at my hearth.

Each turn of year feeds
On my dreams, winter grips my brain
Yet from the flight of birds I read
That seeds of dream will flower again.

Fox Sand

Late Spring Eling wood began, with new growth,
To recover from treefelling but the welts remained.
In that familiar wood I had to find a path
Where before I knew the way.

At first a scratching marked the place
Where the fox came by,
A chaos of feathers and bone stuck to mud,
On fern and against tree bark.

Until this year I had the language pat
Then the landscape convulsed
And everywhere I turned was changed,
Trees fallen, furniture out of place.

Pale green summer glossed the wreckage.
Through the early shade and warm flicker of sun
A shock-ease calmed the wood and unfroze me.

In a dip in a clearing by uprooted plants
I made that fox's digging a point to sit
And shut out the hum of breakage.
I could cope with his mound of sand.

Midsummer I saw among darker green more grit
Freshly dug, more feather and bone litter the clearing.
Flakes of white breast-down began to garland
Fern and bramble.

By late summer the fox had finished.
A skip of sand slid down the bank and his earth
Was large and worn.

Once I saw him sidle through rhododendron roots,
Belly low, bush straight, long nose alive to game.
He had conditioned to change.

I sat at the edge of the clearing
And read the metaphor. I took in his digging
And his lie of trees. The place for fox.

All summer I thought I was watching the wood
Recover and a fox move in. As I sat there I felt
A closed part of me breathe deep.
Hurt was elsewhere.

Early autumn a new fire was built in my cottage,
Set well to fend off winter.
It needed a sand-base to counter heat.

I drove towards a quarry along the road by the wood
Then remembered the fox. I left the car,
Carried a sack into Eling wood to the clearing.
The mound was smoothed by fox play.

I filled the sack with handsfull of sand.
Rabbit, pigeon and pheasant bone I dropped
Where I found them.

The wood is now autumn. The scars are less.
Next season I will know my way by different tracks.

The first fire is ablaze with fox sound.
Sometimes at night I hear in the sand
His hunting screech.

He will be gone next summer.

Cove Cottage, Gurnard's Head

for David Wright

Outside the double window the Atlantic scuds
into the cove and drums an insistent beat
in caves beneath the cottage. Highrise cliffs
are jumping with unneighbourly gulls
while inside the room the noises mingle in frets
of bass and treble that lap and syllable
in my ears as I stare at the breakers
until lulled beyond seeing so the room
is launched and floats out to sea heading,
no chart, no navigation, to the horizon.

i.m. Kit Barker, August 25th 1988

When the foil closed his right eye
a palette as various as landscape
blossomed in his hand. His one
eye took more in, on, and around
the day's season than most
with binoculars or imaged insight.

But the man. O the man.
He could make a sour snake grin,
could coax an old Vanguard another
mile, and talk a day to a standstill.
Apollo's tongue sang from his brushes
and his heart could turn Iceland tropic.

London, Cornwall, America, back
to Sussex; then touring France
and Italy he'd toast the hour with
a homage to wine and church, cheese
and castle, while his eye panned
facade, roof, valley and estuary.

On my wall his painting
of Venice. I can almost hear the city,
see my uncle raise his wine glass.
Then there's Alexander's Head

aslant with one eye smudged—
token to ancient autobiography.

There shall be no epitaph
while memories multiply daily.
I cannot mourn a man imprinted on and
coursing my blood since I was born;
who made grace his chosen bounty
and with grace would quiet harpies.

When I was a boy in Modbury
he'd bring me balsa-modelled
Spitfires and read me sagas.
He gave me my first Austin Seven.
Later, much later, we'd quarter
the country—Cornwall to Highlands.

With sketch-pad and single malt
he'd pen a style from inner eye,
waken the oyster of each day,
exquisite itself, then gently peal
a surge of music from the sea until
sand and cliff echoed with his laugh.

Scraping by; or dropped by
Bond Street galleries I never heard
a whine. He'd aim his tongue at Art
Bureaucracy but was never bitter—
and too generous to be spiteful.
His way? Ignore the worst
and enjoy the rest.

Welcombe Valediction

1
The frontier of going line of love and thunder
like a gold sword appeases lusting blood.
Drown crab and fish, drown.
The rocks are feathered by caress of wave.
We are gone now.
But like the ocean we run different shores

until the moon path leads to this cliff
and all lyrics run dry from weeping.

2

We are gone now.
Sea-things play, urchin, mussel, flat and round fish,
plankton, porpoise, seal, coral, and mermaid,
while our hands explore the nightsea breakers
and peace is far away as a star cupped in a hand.

3

Do not let the nightblack fool you
there is light enough in the fissure of cliff,
cliffs that have to be mounted.
Gone the goat and sheep,
but the buzzard remains.
And blood is inch thick on the road
as it was on steps beneath an altar
when raging Norsemen departed:
buzzards scour the road.
Victim and executioner.

4

This is the wordthought of the seanight
to which we have come out of the maze that douses
cheroot and whirls the aleblur in the brain.
Come, drunken men, the words are hard and dangerous:
Certainly no gain or game.
Look on the sea.
Look on the sea gold with half a moon.

5

Remember the pith and anger which is love
and thunderline is touched by whichever sea
smooths the rocks climbed, sat on, ignored, fished from,
beaten against, stone hurled, and water lapped.
This is the voice that shouts in sunlight,
and in dark moments.
Calls, maybe, from behind smoked glass
close as suntan, and as assailable.

6

The sea furled and ran over rivelled sand.

126

7
The sea gentles the rock in lambwool.
Do not be deceived there is anger.

8
The sea made my right hand sticky Wednesday night
as though I had plunged it wrist deep in blood.

9
The world and sky were mute, and we were deaf.
There could be no sound because ocean and moon were whispering.

10
Still and still and still the beaches are full;
and at night the stars are reflected
by the cigarette
smoked darkly on the cliff top.

11
Bravely we know there can be no departure,
not while a hand is placed in greeting on the water.
This is anciently a seawarrior's greeting
to the departed living, and the dead.
So this image is.

12
Drown crab and fish, drown.
Be damned in the lusting blood,
and severed by a gold sword,
crushed under white rock,
and wept for in lyrics.

Move over minute things in pools of water.

Nothing moved but these figures
a multiplication of three dark shapes
that held silence in the night.

We are gone now.